This book is a gift for:

From:

For:

Bible Stories
for Toddlers

Best-Loved Bible Stories
in Rhyme

Text: Tomasz Kruczek
Illustrator: Magda Bloch

christian
art kids

Originally published under the title: *BIBLIJNE WYCIECZKI ZUZI OWIECZKI*
Copyright © 2008 by VOCATIO
Published under license of VOCATIO, e-mail: wydawca@vocatio.com.pl
3941 E. Chandler Blvd. Suite 106-106
Phoenix, AZ 85048, USA

Text and artwork copyright © 2010 by VOCATIO

Translated by: The Czopek Family who dedicate this translation to James and
Yohan Sonoda and all their little friends in Antakya, Turkey.

Copyright © 2011 by Christian Art Kids, an imprint of Christian Art Publishers,
PO Box 1599, Vereeniging, 1930, RSA

1025 N Lombard Road, Lombard, IL, 60148, USA

First edition 2011

Printed in China

ISBN 978-1-77036-848-4

11   12   13   14   15   16   17   18   19   20   –   10 9 8 7 6 5 4 3 2 1

Table of Contents

Old Testament

New Testament

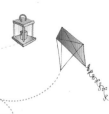

From Creation through Ancient Times

Introduction

Did you know there is a book
God has given to us all
So that we can have a look
How to walk and where to go?

It's the Bible! You guessed right!
Full of wisdom straight from Him.
It will fill your soul with light!
It will fill it to the brim!

Many nights and many days
Wise men penned what God had said,
Now the Book shows us the way
Through each smile and each tear shed.

All these pictures are for you;
They're so pretty, can you see?
All these stories tell the truth
And that truth will set you free.

Rhymes are so much fun to read.
You can't read yet? Don't be sad!
Grab the book, that's all you need,
Hand it to your mom or dad!

"What's the big deal?" you might say.
Let me tell you, my dear friend;
Those who follow this Book's ways
Will find new life in the end.

Creation

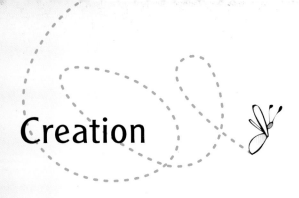

Back when God was all alone
There was nothing else around,
Nothing but God on His throne!
Now, how crazy does that sound?

Then God spoke and with His breath
Out of nothing came to be
Darkness, light, heavens and earth!
That's amazing, you agree?

Now the time came to give names
To the darkness and the light,
So God called the light "a day"
And the dark He called "a night".

Out of all the waters' flow,
God made gorgeous skies up high.
He put rivers down below
And another day went by.

Rivers, oceans, lakes and seas
Open up to show the land.
Flowers, bushes, grass and trees
All turn green at God's command.

Third day comes, but God's not done;
He makes millions of bright stars.
Then He adds the Moon, the Sun,
All the planets, even Mars!

Day Four must have been so loud!
Critters popped up everywhere!
Just imagine all that crowd!
On the ground and in the air!

On Day Five, the earth brought forth
All the creatures from within;
Little things of every sort
Came out to be counted in.

On Day Six God worked again
And He thought of something new;
He created the first people:
Man and woman, they were two!

God gave them eternal life
Full of happiness and grace;
The first husband and his wife
In this glorious, lovely place.

In six days God made this world
With His power and His might.
It was pleasing to the Lord
And brought joy into His heart.

When the seventh day arrived
God thought, "Wow! I'm done! Hurray!"
He looked at His work and smiled,
And enjoyed a holiday.

Adam and Eve

Close your eyes and think of this:
Life with nothing but sweet joy,
Pleasure, happiness and bliss.
Wouldn't that be great? Oh, boy!

That's what Adam and Eve had
In the garden God had made.
Always joyous, never sad,
Not a thing made them afraid.

He and she in paradise
Among flowers, fruits, and trees.
Up above the clear blue skies,
Perfect harmony and peace.

Just like father and his son,
God took Adam for a walk.
First He showed him what He'd done,
Then He also gave him work.

"Dress and keep this garden here,"
Was the Lord's direct command.
"But don't touch that tree, you hear?
If you do, you will be dead."

All the other trees were fine
To enjoy and pick the fruit.
This one had knowledge divine
Of what's bad and what is good.

Now, the serpent crawled right by
And that's what he said to Eve,
"Try the fruit, you will not die!"
Oh, poor Eve, she was deceived!

On and on the crafty snake
Whispered sweetly in her ear.
Will she make this huge mistake,
Even though God's word was clear?

Eve looked at the tree's delight,
Her mind was made up within.
Grabbed the fruit then took a bite,
Thus committing the first sin.

Later Adam had a taste
Of the fruit that had been banned;
Broke the law that God had placed,
Disobeyed his Lord's command.

Now their eyes were opened wide
And their hearts were filled with fear.
From their God they tried to hide,
For they knew that He was near.

Once with God, in peace and joy,
Love was theirs to share each day.
Now, the harmony destroyed;
Now, two people gone astray.

The first people's life got much harder
When God told them they must leave.
They could not live in the garden;
Shame on Adam, shame on Eve.

That's how sin came to this earth,
Because Adam and Eve disobeyed.
Evil entered, with it death,
And destroyed what God had made.

14

The Flood

Do you like when rain falls down
And the clouds cover the sky?
Here's a story about how
Tons of water came up high.

Long ago, in ancient days,
Men were badly misbehaved.
For their sins and their disgrace
God would send a huge, mean wave.

But the flood would spare one man.
Noah — have you heard that name?
He loved God, and in God's plan
Noah would not face the shame.

He would soon build a big ship
Because that was God's command.
In it he would take a trip
To find rescue on dry land.

Other people laughed so hard
When he gathered all the wood.
"When's the flood going to start?"
They joked and scoffed all they could.

Did the jokes make Noah worried?
Not a chance; this man was brave.
He told all his sons to hurry
If they wanted to be saved.

When the ark was finally done,
All the critters got inside.
No pair left, not even one;
They kept coming from each side.

Big ones, small ones, every size.
Some were friendly, some were wild.
But — here comes the big surprise —
To each other they were kind.

Mammals, reptiles, and birds too;
Each was needed, Noah said.
But mosquitoes? Why those two?
Oh, why not? Go right ahead!

When the earth became a sea,
All those in the ark were fine.
Thanks to Noah, who believed
In the promise so divine.

Through the many days of rain,
The big boat would float around.
Noah looked, but all in vain,
As he tried to find dry ground.

But the rain came to an end
And so Noah sent a dove
To look for a piece of land,
A sign of God's amazing love.

Good news! Water has come down!
A big mount came into sight.
Noah's ark stops at its crown,
And the sky is clear and bright!

Out the ark they all jump out,
Shouting gladly in sun's rays.
Nobody now thinks about
All the sadness of past days.

They all look up to the sky
And see something from the Lord;
There's a rainbow, way up high,
Sign that God has kept His word.

Rainbow is a promise made
To all people in this world,
That God will come to our aid
If we love Him and His word.

19

The Tower of Babel

The flood's waters had gone down;
People journeyed far and near,
And they started building towns.
Listen to what happened here.

Shinar was a piece of land
That some folks liked really well;
So they built hard, hand in hand,
A town in which they could dwell.

They made bricks out of big stones
And worked hard to see them rise.
Even though it hurt their bones,
They built on and liked large size.

But soon pride entered their hearts;
When they walked around to see
Their new town and all its parts.
Everyone thought, "Me, me, me!"

"Look at us, we are so smart!"
They said smiling, standing tall.
"We can have a whole new start,
We don't need God, not at all."

"We can build better and more,
Stronger, mightier, and way high!
Let us start a brand-new chore;
Build a tower to the sky!"

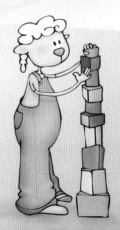

"Let us give it a great name,
Name above all names, indeed,
So that others know our fame,
The whole world we want to lead!"

God saw all this and looked down
At the tower tall and strong
And their big and shiny town,
But He knew that it was wrong.

Why? Because they thought they could
Reach the heaven by their feet;
They surely misunderstood,
This would end in their defeat.

Then God looked at all the rest
And it made Him really sad,
For they did not do their best
With the knowledge that they had.

"You can't live like that, My dear,
Bragging about your own skill.
You've worked hard, and that is clear,
But you cared not for My will!"

So God mixed their tongues right then,
Causing all the work to stop.
Though they tried and tried again,
Conversation was a flop.

They can't understand a word
It's a feeling rather strange,
Just imagine that you heard
This whole story – but in French!

Now, years later people speak
Many languages, no doubt:
Polish, Japanese and Greek.
How many? You should find out!

Abraham

Here's a story from a place
Where the sun dries up the land.
It's a huge and open space
Called a desert, full of sand.

Abram lived there, have you heard?
An old man with hair that's gray;
God had given him this word:
"Get up and move far away.

I will give you your own land
If you promise to obey,
And your nation will expand;
You will be blessed in your day!"

Abram gathered all the folk,
They packed everything they had;
Some thought, "Maybe it's a joke?
Is the old man going mad?"

It was not a joke at all;
It was faith that Abram showed
To respond to his God's call
As they traveled the long road.

But a worry soon crept in
When the journey was all done.
Abram became sad within
Growing old without a son.

His wife, Sarah, also sad,
Knew she too was at the age
When a child could not be had;
Not by her, not at this stage.

But God had another plan.
He told Abram, "Look up, friend.
Through faith in Me you began;
Through this same faith you will end!"

25

"ABRAHAM is now your name,
Just as all the stars above
Many children you will claim
Because of My might and love."

Weeks and months have come and gone,
But Abraham did not doubt;
He believed and waited
On God's promise to come about.

Abraham was out one day
Next to his and Sarah's tent;
Three visitors walked that way.
Were they angels that God sent?

Yes, indeed, from God they came!
For them it was close, not far.
They must have things to proclaim,
Let us see just who they are.

"Abraham," they said with joy,
"Just like God promised to you,
You will have a little boy.
Now believe, for this is true!"

Sarah, when she heard the news
That the angels came and told,
Was surprised, even amused,
For she knew that she was old.

But we know that in His might
God can bring about His will,
And to Sarah's sweet delight,
His great promise He fulfilled.

God made everything work out
For Abraham and his wife;
You will soon learn more about
Isaac's adventurous life.

A Wife for Isaac

In this story God will test
Both Abraham and his son;
Will God be sad or impressed?
Find out when the story's done.

"Take Isaac with you and go
To the mountains high," God said.
"When you get there, you will know
What to do, now go ahead!"

On the mountain there's a fire
Father and his son are there,
Now an offer is required
That the father must prepare.

The time of the test is here!
Abraham must kill his son!
But God told him, "Stop and hear!
Kill a lamb, and spare this one!"

So Abraham passed the test,
God was pleased for he obeyed.
Isaac will live and be blessed,
God has come to this boy's aid.

Later, when Isaac grew tall,
His dad said, "You have your life,
So a servant we will call
To go find you a good wife."

Off the servant went to look
For the most suitable dame;
Every corner, every nook,
Every kind, and every name.

He thought, "It's no easy task!
There are many girls that fit!
Where to go next? Whom to ask?
I feel like I want to quit."

But instead, the servant prayed,
Asking God to give him grace:
"Help me, Lord, for I'm afraid
This could be a hopeless case!

I will go stand by the well
Where the girls with buckets come,
Will You help me, Lord, to tell
Which one should the wife become?

If I ask her for a drink
For my camel and for me,
And she will not even think,
But to help she will agree,

I will see it as a sign
That she truly is the one,
With Your perfect will divine
My long mission will be done."

As he finished praying, there
Came Rebekah, a young miss.
Why, her beauty was so rare,
Looking at her was bliss!

The servant said, as he planned,
"Give me water, will you dear?"
Right away she stretched her hand
"Drink up," she said full of cheer.

"You are thirsty! That is true!
But your camels also are;
I will give them water too.
You must have come from afar!"

Now the servant knew she was
The girl that God had in view,
And she went with him because
She was a believer, too.

Jacob and Esau

There once were two little brothers,
They were twins, to be exact.
Did one look just like the other?
Strangely not, and that's a fact!

Esau wasn't born too cute;
He was covered in thick hair.
Jacob grasping Esau's foot,
Breathing his first gasp of air.

In those times the firstborn son
Was more special than the rest;
He was chosen as the one
Whom his father gladly blessed.

But the blessing would not last
Without hard work to be done.
Life would not be just a blast
For the oldest, firstborn son.

One day Esau came back home
And saw Jacob eating lunch.
"I am starved," he loudly moaned,
"Save my life and let me munch!"

"Have this good soup," Jacob said,
"But your birthright is my pay!"
"You can have it. Go ahead!"
Esau ate his right away.

One time Esau's aging dad
Told him to come very near,
"My son, this is very sad,
But I'll soon be gone from here.

And before I leave this world
I would like to bless you, child.
So I now want you to go
Bring me game from forest wild."

But when Jacob heard his father,
He decided he would cheat;
Looking just like his own brother,
Off he went to his dad's feet.

The old man's eyes were very sick,
He did not know what he saw;
Jacob played a dirty trick –
Stole the blessing from Esau.

As you probably can guess,
Esau became very mad:
"Brother, you've made such a mess!
I just want to kill you now!"

Jacob had to run and hide,
Wandering both far and deep;
Once when he got sleepy eyed
He saw these things in his sleep:

Many angels on a ladder
Climbing low and climbing high;
One angel after another,
All the way up to the sky.

And he saw the Lord Himself
Standing up above it all:
"I am God!" He loudly said,
"And I will not let you fall."

Jacob woke up at the dawn,
Filled with fear and full of awe;
All his disobedience gone
With the dream that he just saw.

God made everything anew
Because Jacob went his way,
And he got a new name too –
Israel – easy to say!

Joseph

In this story you will read
That this life Is sometimes rough;
And it's full of strife and greed,
Not to mention other stuff.

Joseph (you can call him Joe)
Had a bunch of brothers, and
As you soon will see below,
They were not the best of friends.

God gave special dreams to Joe,
But not to the other fellows.
In them, future things were shown
Joseph's brothers were so jealous!

Things did not turn for the best
When the boys got gifts from Dad,
Joe's was better than the rest –
Older brothers were so mad!

So mad were they, that they sold
Their young brother to some men;
He would now travel the world
As a slave in caravan.

Joe worked hard for his new lord
In Egyptian foreign land;
For this he got a reward
And became his lord's right hand.

But it's strange, this life of ours;
Sometimes bad things come our way –
Joseph ends up behind bars,
Though he did not go astray.

Meanwhile, Pharaoh, Joseph's master
Has a dream sent him from God.
In it he sees a disaster;
Things he dream are pretty odd.

He woke up distressed and said,
"What a nightmare! Scary scenes!
I must get out of my bed
And find out what it all means!"

Dreams were no secret to Joe
(God was with him, don't forget!).
To his lord he said, "Hello,"
And then added "Do not fret."

"Seven years of full, rich crop
Are awaiting, it appears.
Then the time of wealth will stop
For another seven years."

Joseph's life was changed again!
It's now great, though it was tough.
In the palace he would reign,
And take care of lots of stuff.

First he gave a big command,
"Go and gather all the wheat!
When the famine hits the land
We will have plenty to eat."

Soon thereafter, big surprise,
Joseph's brothers came to town
Looking for some food supplies
Would their brother let them down?

Joseph realized that God's plan
Was to send him to this place
And to show him he's the man
Who forgives and offers grace.

When his brothers came for food,
He forgave them all their sins.
God made things between them good
And he made them best of friends.

Moses

There's a river long and wide,
Far in the Egyptian land;
Let this story be your guide
As we go there, hand in hand.

Do you see a basket there
Flowing down the river wild?
Why, this sight is truly rare,
In the basket is a child!

Little Moses is his name
Full of tears in his small eyes,
For his mommy put him there
To protect him from bad guys.

Pharaoh's daughter passed by
Noticed the boy unknown
She thought, "Oh, no! He could die!"
Rescued him to be her own.

Baby Moses grew up fast,
Well taught near pyramids high,
But his good life did not last –
You will quickly find out why.

One day an Egyptian guard
Beat a harmless Israelite.
Moses hit him back so hard
Killing him, forcing his flight.

His life went from good to bad
He was filled with fear and shame.
To kill someone? That's so sad!
He would never be the same.

Moses had to flee and hide,
Change to become a new man.
Once a prince, a shepherd now
All because of God's plan.

His work now was tending sheep
Living with his wife and kids,
But some nights he couldn't sleep
When he thought of what he did.

One time, on a sunny day,
Moses worked in his pasture
When he saw far, far away
Bush on fire, that's for sure!

Flames were big and fiery red,
Undamaged bush was explored.
Then a voice from heaven said,
"Please come, Moses, I'm your Lord!"

"I have watched My people's pain
And will now extend My hand
So that Israel can now gain
And settle in a new land.

Many wonders you will see
By My power, do not doubt,
Back to Egypt you'll soon be;
Aaron too will help you out."

Moses listened to God's plan,
God's purpose so plain to see,
That with His help he now can
Go to make his people free.

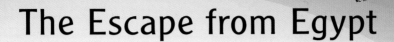

The Escape from Egypt

Have you read it? Have you heard?
About Moses who's so brave?
How according to God's word,
His own people he would save?

Off to Egypt Moses went
And his brother came along,
They are there to represent
Peoples to which they belong.

They want all Jews to be free
And that freedom they will seek,
But bad Pharaoh won't agree
He wants Israel to be weak.

Jumping frogs and flying flies,
People getting very ill.
God is sending warning signs,
But they don't break Pharaoh's will.

He keeps saying, "No, no way!"
He won't let God's children go.
There's a new plague every day
Yet his answer's always "No!"

But God has a lot more power
To defeat bad Pharaoh's schemes
Firstborn sons die at one hour –
Egypt is filled with loud screams.

Jewish firstborn sons were spared
Through the blood marks on their doors;
They are safe at home to share
A special meal, and not God's curse.

Moses walks on solid ground;
Twelve tribes follow hand in hand.
God's great power hovers round
As they head towards new land.

To the desert they now go
Out of Egypt, slaves no more,
Though their confidence is low,
They're much happier than before.

Pharaoh's face took on a frown
Seeing wonders God has done.
He tells soldiers, "Chase them down!"
Right toward the sea they run.

Pharaoh in his crazy rage
Sends his armies on a chase,
He is seeking his revenge.
Will his army win the race?

But the passage closed up fast
For the evil army's feet;
Their wild chase sure did not last,
They all drowned and met defeat.

Israelites are full of fear,
Stuck between their foes and sea.
Moses prays and he's sincere,
He asks God to help them flee.

All God's children are secure,
Raging sea behind their backs.
Egypt, once so strong and sure,
Is no more — they can relax.

The Lord's glory is made known
When we pray and trust in Him.
To the sides are sea's waves blown,
People now can walk, not swim.

Music is playing, drums and bells;
They praise God, they sing and shout.
To the whole world this noise tells:
God's the winner! There's no doubt!

Joshua

When vacation time is close
And it's time to hit the road,
You must fill your bags with clothes
And then get ready to load.

But imagine, if you can,
How your parents would react
To a trip with a long plan –
Forty years to be exact.

God's own people once set out
On a trip through desert's sand;
Though their hearts were filled with doubt,
They marched to the Promised Land.

The new land was green and lush;
Full of rich and tasty crop.
But they feared, they didn't rush
On the road they often stopped.

Many dangers on the way
Caused their faith to become weak.
Someone old died every day
And their hope was looking bleak.

Joshua and Caleb, both
With the ones who stayed alive;
Forty years pursued God's oath
Till they finally arrived.

When they ended their long trip,
Joshua became their chief;
Now his job was to equip
The Lord's nation to believe.

Once a city, huge and strong,
Posed a danger to their land;
It had big walls all along
And was ruled by a mighty hand.

Jericho was this town's name
Its fortress was hard to climb.
No one had destroyed its fame;
Could this now be the first time?

Joshua sends men to spy;
They sneak through the city gate.
Once inside they almost die,
But a woman saves their fate.

Now it's time for God to scheme
And to bring the city down.
Joshua summons his team;
They are gathering around.

Seven days they are to walk,
But no need for arrows, bows.
Seven days, around the clock —
Will they win? God surely knows!

As they're walking round and round,
Priests are carrying the Lord's ark;
In the air the trumpets sound
Through the day and in the dark.

On the last, the seventh day,
As instructed by the Lord,
They marched seven times and prayed
And then yelled in one accord.

They yelled as loud as they could
And God surely did His part.
Jericho no longer stood;
The whole city fell apart.

That's how Jericho was won
Because God was on their side.
We too can get great things done
If in God we do abide.

Samson

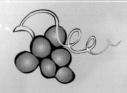

Being strong is really cool,
But you also must be wise.
For the one who is a fool,
Many problems will arise.

There once was a man of might
Whose strong arms came from the Lord,
But some things he did weren't right –
Here's the story, word for word:

Samson was the young lad's name
And his strength was known to all;
His big muscles were his fame,
He was big and very tall.

One time Samson heard a roar,
A big lion jumped at him!
Was he scared? Oh, not at all!
Lion's chances were too slim.

Why was Samson super strong?
Read and try to understand:
It's because his hair was long!
Following the Lord's command.

When the time came for a fight
Samson fully trusted God
To provide His Spirit's might,
Which is awesome and unflawed.

People called the Philistines
Lived back then close to the Jews
And they hated them, which means
There would never be a truce.

Samson was the chosen man
To defeat all of God's foes,
When the fighting soon began
He just knocked them off their toes.

But his strength would fade away
When he met a lovely dame;
She would soon lead him astray,
Sweet Delilah was her name.

Samson did not know one thing:
This girl was a clever spy
Hired by the Philistines
To ask questions: What? How? Why?

She asked why he was so strong,
Why this, what's that, why long hair?
And though it was very wrong,
He revealed the truth to her.

When he slept the bad men came
And they cut his hair off fast.
Samson became too weak and lame
And they captured him at last.

Samson's hair did grow again,
But his eyes could see no more
Once they took him in his chain
Where their false gods were adored.

One more time God's power shone
Through blind Samson's awesome might,
He destroyed the bad men's home;
They were crushed and Samson died.

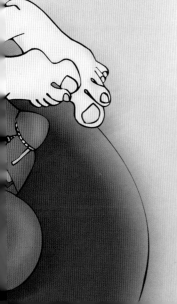

Ruth and Naomi

This next story, my dear friends,
Might seem sad to all of you,
But to find out how it ends,
Listen, because it is true!

Let me take you to a place
Which is very far from here.
Meet Naomi. See her face?
Down her cheek there flows a tear.

She is sad, her husband died
Her sons died too, leaving wives.
Now they all have to decide
How to go on with their lives.

Her son's wife, whose name is Ruth
Makes a promise not to leave:
"I will help you, it's the truth,
We will get through all this grief."

"Even though we are so poor
I will always be with you
God will help us to endure
He will surely see us through!"

Off to Bethlehem they go
In the far Judean land,
To a place where long ago
A nice farm house used to stand.

But there isn't much left now,
Just a field, a few square feet;
Should they work the land and plow?
Sell it so that they can eat?

When the harvest time was near
Lots of barley grew around,
Ruth worked hard until each ear
Was soon gathered from the ground.

An old Jewish custom said
That some crops were to be spared
For the poor, to give them bread,
And to show them that God cared.

Boaz, who managed that land
Told his servants to leave more,
That from his generous hand
God could help those who were poor.

Soon when Boaz and Ruth met
She told him about her life
Right away his mind was set,
He would have her as his wife.

Though the story started sad,
A happy end is surely near;
Soon a wedding will be had
Full of joy and not one tear.

Boaz bought more farming land
And – you guessed it – wedding rings!
Then he married Ruth, as planned
And shared with her all the things.

Soon more laughter filled the air,
Ruth and Boaz had a son!
O, how God had shown His care
Through the miracles He'd done!

Samuel

Here is another story
That I would now like to tell
About God and His glory
And things not going so well.

God's children in His nation
Were selfish and full of sin,
They lacked the dedication
And were not humble within.

Among them lived a small boy
Who was well behaved and smart,
By a priest he was employed
And worked hard to earn his part.

He was born against all odds,
And to show her gratitude
His mom gave him to be God's
And to learn good attitude.

One night he was lying down,
Someone loudly called his name:
"Samuel!" – he looked around,
"Here I am!" Samuel claimed.

To the priest he quickly goes
(Eli is his name, you see):
"You must need me, I suppose?
Do you have a chore for me?"

But the priest is caught off guard
"Young man, there is nothing wrong.
I did not call, I slept hard,
Go to bed now, run along!"

Samuel returns to bed
And he tries to sleep at last,
But he hears the voice instead
He returns to Eli fast!

"Samuel, I did not call,"
Says the priest surprised once more,
"I did not get up at all,
I need rest, so close the door."

Just as soon as his eyes shut
That same voice was again heard,
So the boy does you know what
And he feels a bit absurd.

That's when Eli understood
It was God's voice in the night
"Young man," he said, "it'll be good
If you hear and do what's right."

And it happened in that way
God spoke to the boy once more,
Samuel would now obey.
The Lord's voice was not ignored.

In those tough times long ago
Samuel learned one thing well:
When God calls you, you should go
At His service to excel.

After many years went by
And Samuel grew to be a man,
God said to him from on high
"I have yet another plan!"

Two kings I will soon appoint,
One is David, one is Saul,
You'll be the one to anoint
Both of them with special oil.

What can we learn from this all?
I am very glad you asked:
Even though you may be small,
God will bless you with a task!

David

This new story is about
David, man of world-wide fame.
His adventures are, no doubt,
Worthy to be now proclaimed.

David, when he was still small,
Tended sheep day after day;
Summer, winter, spring or fall
He would walk them far away.

One night, when the moon was bright,
A wild lion scared the sheep;
David wasn't too polite
Killed the lion, earned his keep.

David worshiped his Lord, too,
Playing harp the best he could;
This is how the Lord God knew
That his service would be good.

At that time there was a fight,
Evil armies everywhere,
And Goliath, a huge knight
Of whom everyone was scared.

Why? Because he was so strong!
So enormous, with great skill!
And his sword was sharp and long,
Ready to hurt and to kill.

Just then David came to town
From his job of tending flock,
Why was everyone so down?
By Goliath they were mocked!

David saw Goliath's grin
And he heard him laugh so loud.
He became angry within
"I will fight him!" the boy vowed.

David goes to his king's tent.
Eager to fight with his all.
"Is he whom our God has sent?"
King asks and says, "Boy, you're small!"

"I'll go to the battlefield!"
David wants to be in charge
But he can't lift up the shield,
And the armor? It's too large!

But who needs a shield or sword
When God says His help is near?
David's strength is in the Lord
In Him he will persevere.

David is now on the battleground
Holding slingshot in his hands.
Peace and courage do abound
In his heart, with God he stands.

All it took was one smooth stone
And the evil armies fled,
That one rock David had thrown
Struck Goliath on the head.

Israel is full of joy!
People dance and shout and sing,
God has used a faithful boy
Who would later be the king.

Solomon

In the Bible it is told
Of a king who acted wise.
He had lots and lots of gold
And he loved to give advice.

The king's name was Solomon
And believe me when I say,
That his equals there were none
Neither close nor far away.

As the king, he had it all —
Servants, friends and armies too.
All his knights were strong and tall,
He was mighty through and through.

When God came to him at night
Asking him to choose a gift,
He chose wisdom, now, that's bright!
But that's not all he received.

God was pleased with such a choice
So the king received much more,
Solomon could now rejoice
He was richer than before.

He raised temples and wrote books
Thanks to him justice was served.
Sometimes he would punish crooks
People got what they deserved.

Once two ladies broke the calm
Fighting for a little child,
Each one said she was the mom
Things became a little wild.

One says, "Give the child to me!"
But the other says the same!
Back and forth, they can't agree;
What a sad scene, what a shame!

King Solomon, being smart
Knew exactly what to do:
"Shall we cut the child apart
And give half to each of you?"

The first mother says, "Okay!"
Second one gets on her knees,
"No! I'll give the child away!
Let her have my baby, please!"

Solomon decides the case,
"She's the mother, now I know!
I'll extend to her my grace,
But the other has to go!"

Solomon made up his mind
And the baby's life was spared,
To the true mom he was kind
When he saw how much she cared.

Now the mom was with her child
And the king showed to be wise,
Everyone rejoiced and smiled
No one argued, no one cried.

It is good when you and I
Ask for wisdom from above;
If we pray, God will supply
He gives freely in His love.

Esther

There once was a festive king
Who was looking for a wife;
Celebrating was his thing
To enjoy and share in life.

In his kingdom, big and wide
There lived Jewish people too.
With them Esther, a young bride,
And her uncle, a great Jew.

Out of all the girls in town
That the king could choose to wed,
Esther was the prettiest one
"I will marry her," he said.

When before the king she stood
In her most beautiful dress,
He asked her whether she would
Marry him, and she said "Yes!"

Do you think this story's done
Because Esther is a queen?
No! The trouble's just begun!
Read on to see what I mean.

In the king's court was a man,
Haman, he was proud and vain;
In his head he had a plan,
What's the plan? Let me explain.

He told people to bow down,
As they saw him walking by
But one day he had to frown
Because he met Mordecai.

Esther's uncle (yes, that's him)
Did not bow, made Haman mad,
Now his future's looking grim
Haman wants revenge so bad!

He begins to spread the lie
That the Jews are the king's foes
And that all of them should die —
Will his mean lie be exposed?

Mordecai cannot believe
What his brave act brought about;
He can't stop to cry and grieve
Asking God to help him out.

Esther sees her uncle's tears,
"What's the matter? Please, do tell."
"We shall die," Mordecai fears,
"You might lose your life as well."

Esther answers, "You must pray,
To our God who's on the throne.
Meanwhile, I will find a way
To speak with the king alone."

To the king she goes in fear
Trying to be sweet, polite.
"I'm inviting you, my dear
To a lovely feast tonight."

O, the King ate and had fun!
He thanked Esther and then said,
"My dear, what would you like done?
Please, do tell me, go ahead."

Esther takes a long, deep breath,
"I'm a Jewish girl, you see.
Your man, Haman, he wants death
For my people, and for me."

Will the king save his own wife?
Yes! He's angry, and he's just!
Haman's lies cost him his life,
And his pride turned into dust.

Jonah

To His servant God once said,
(Jonah was his name, you know),
"I've got news for you to spread
Will you get ready and go?"

"Go where?" Jonah asked his Lord,
"To Nineveh," God replied,
"Where My word has been ignored
and the hearts are filled with pride."

"Tell the people that their sin
Makes Me sad and sick at heart.
The repentance must begin,
Week-long sorrow they must start."

Jonah frowned and thought, "Oh, no!
What am I supposed to say?
I don't really want to go,
Bad idea! Can't! No way!"

Then it dawns on him, "Oh, yes!
I will travel far away,
I don't think I need this stress
I will board a ship today!"

Jonah's crafty scheme unfolds
As he hops onto the boat
"Welcome! Ship ahoy!" he's told,
"Buckle up and let us float!"

Soon the blue skies turn to black
And the waves rage all about,
Thunder strikes with a loud CRACK!
Everyone begins to shout.

"Why the sudden weather change?"
Sailors cannot understand,
"This indeed is very strange,
Must be the Almighty's hand."

Jonah knows he is to blame
He says, "It's because of me!
I have sinned, oh, what a shame!"
And he's tossed into the sea!

But the story doesn't end
Thanks to a humongous fish,
Whom God very quickly sends
To have Jonah for a dish.

Three whole days inside the whale
Jonah cries out to his Lord,
"Please, forgive me that I failed!
I will change, I give my word!"

God heard Jonah's earnest plea
And the fish heard this command:
"Let My servant now go free,
Spit him out on a dry land."

Jonah knew where he should run –
To Nineveh, to the King
Bring them news that sin's no fun;
Tell them sin's an ugly thing.

When the people in that town
Listened to what Jonah spoke,
All they could do was to frown
Because God's law was no joke.

Grown-ups, teens, and children too
Hoped the Lord would show them pity;
Their repentance was so true,
God was glad to spare their city.

All the sins that they had done
God forgave them with a smile.
Many new lives were begun
Jonah's journey was worthwhile.

Daniel

Even though he was a slave
As a boy and then young man,
Daniel showed that he was brave
And had faith in God's great plan.

This took place in Babylon;
Israelites were captives there,
But their lives had to go on
As they trusted in God's care.

When he was a little kid
Daniel had to go to school.
Did he like it? Yes, he did!
Learning things is really cool!

Someone soon heard Daniel say
He would never eat the things
That would make him disobey
God's commands and not the king's.

"I will not eat royal food,"
Daniel promised in his mind.
Now his diet would include
Fruit and veggies of all kind.

Daniel grew up strong and wise,
And he got a royal task:
To the king he would advise;
He did well and learned quite fast!

In his job he would explain
Dreams the ruler had at night.
Others tried it, but in vain;
Only Daniel got them right.

His foes said, "Daniel must pay!"
So they gave the king this thought,
"You should make the people pray
To you only, not their God."

They did that because they knew
Daniel would never obey;
He would bow to no one who
Would make people go astray.

Prayer time for Daniel came;
Everyone could hear him clear.
He was calling on God's name
Without any shame or fear.

His foes caught him in the act;
To the throne they went again,
And the king had to react:
"Throw him in the lions' den!"

Oh, the king was rather sad,
But he had to keep his laws.
Daniel's jealous foes were glad
When they saw the lions' paws.

Would the Lord let Daniel die?
No! He sent His angel down.
Now the beasts seem very shy;
Daniel smiles, the lions frown.

All night long, down in the hole
Daniel spent, but stayed alive.
Did his foes' schemes work at all?
No, with God's help he survived.

The New
Adventures

The New Adventures

Do you know or have you heard
That for thousands of years long
People waited for God's word
To finally come along?

When the first people had sinned
Separation had begun,
But God promised to send
The Messiah, His own Son.

He will save the human race
And bring God's peace to this earth.
Through His love and by His grace
People will gain back their worth.

It is time to read about
God's Son who comes from above
So that people can find out
About His power and His love.

He gives life that's fresh and new
Full of riches to bestow.
Jesus does that! Yes, it's true!
It is Him you'll get to know.

Come along and we will go
On a journey, you and I,
Where together we can grow
And see glory up on high.

Prepare the Way

You are now about to hear
A great story, my dear friend,
So make sure to lend your ear
And please listen to the end.

Back when Herod was a king
Lived a priest whose job was to
Serve his God in everything
And to offer Him what's due.

One day the Lord's angel came,
"Zechariah, hear!" he said
"Your son will one day proclaim
The salvation that's ahead!"

Zechariah said in shock,
"We're too old to have a son,
We cannot turn back the clock,
Some things cannot be undone!"

"You will not speak by God's choice,"
Said the angel, "but don't fret,
He will give you back your voice
When the time for it is set."

Zechariah tries to speak,
But he can't say words, not one.
And his wife, though old and weak,
By God's grace carries a son.

Her name is Elizabeth;
Soon she bears a baby boy.
As he catches his first breath,
Everyone is full of joy.

What will be the baby's name?
Everybody wants to know.
"John," the proud parents proclaim,
"To prepare the way he'll go."

When the boy became a man,
Off to wilderness he went.
That's when he truly began
The task for which he was sent.

"Make the paths straight for the Lord,"
That was John's gentle command.
"Do not sin and be restored,
For God's kingdom is at hand!"

Who's the Lord? It's God's own Son!
In Him life anew begins.
Through Him great things will be done.
He will save us from our sins!

Crowds came and they heard John preach
About God's love and His ways;
No one was outside the reach
Of God's mercy and His grace.

Many said that they believed
Their lives changed, and as a sign,
A baptism they did receive.
And God said, "Now you are Mine."

Who did John come to proclaim?
Do you know or can you guess?
Your life will not be the same,
Find out and you will be blessed!

Mary and Joseph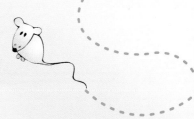

When God sends His angel down,
You know that you should beware.
He sent one to a small town,
To young Mary who lived there.

You will bear a baby son,
He will grow to be the King.
God in flesh, the Chosen One;
Love and justice He will bring.

"Peace to you, o full of grace!
God is with you on this day."
He told Mary, and her face
Showed surprise, she thought, "No way!"

"How can this even be true?"
Mary asked very surprised.
"Holy Ghost will come to you,
Just trust God for He is wise."

Gabriel was the angel's name
And he gave Mary this news:
"I am here to proclaim
You're the one God wants to choose.

Humbled, young Mary replied,
"May it be just as you say!
In my God I will abide,
And I will gladly obey."

Joseph, Mary's fiancé,
When he learned what had gone on
Wanted to go far away
For the child was not his son.

But the angel came and said,
"Mary's son comes from above
God wants you and her to wed,"
Joseph stayed and showed her love.

As the birth is coming near
There is trouble in the air,
Caesar wants to count this year
All the people who live there.

That's what rulers sometimes do;
What they order, must be done.
Grown-ups, youngsters, babies too
Will be counted, one by one.

Off to Bethlehem they go,
The young couple, hand in hand
Through the valleys and down low
Through hot sun and desert sand.

Now they reach the city's gate;
Mary's time is coming near.
Things seem to go well, but ... wait!
There is no room for them here!

They stop in at a little inn,
But no beds are to be found;
Soon the cold night will begin
Darkness hangs above the ground.

At last! There's a barn with hay!
Under stars and shiny moon,
What comes next, I will not say;
You will find out very soon!

92

The Birth of Jesus

Bethlehem turned off the lights,
Everyone is sound asleep;
Only shepherds in the night
Take care of their many sheep.

They work long and they work hard
Every night they tend their fold.
Taking turns to be on guard
In the dark and sometimes cold.

Suddenly, a shining light
Fills the darkness of the sky,
It's God's angel, what a sight!
Coming down from up on high!

"Don't be scared!" his voice commands
As the shepherds look in fear,
"I want you to understand
That the Savior has appeared.

In the city of the king,
Christ was born this very day.
So rejoice! Praise God and sing!
God has shown His love today!

Praise the Lord our God of love
Peace to everyone on earth!"
Sang the angels up above,
Celebrating the Son's birth.

"Let us go to that great place,"
Said the shepherds filled with awe,
"See the Savior face to face
And tell others what we saw."

Off to Bethlehem they go
To find Baby Jesus there,
Promised by God long ago
Now under His parents' care.

Wise Men from the eastern lands
When they heard of the whole thing,
They traveled through the sands
To see Herod, then, the king.

"We have traveled from afar
For the newborn King of Jews.
Following a big, bright star
We thought you would have some news."

Herod, jealous and annoyed
Told the wise men on the side,
"I too want to greet the boy,
Can you tell Him I said hi?"

"On your way back, do stop by
Tell me how to find the place."
Herod wants the child to die,
What a shame! What a disgrace!

So the wise men went away,
Following the star again.
Through the night and through the day
In the sun and in the rain.

They brought gifts to show their joy —
Frankincense and myrrh and gold,
And they gave them to the boy
But Herod was never told.

The Son of God

Let us travel yet once more
To where Jordan river flows;
Here's John, just like before
Preaching about what he knows.

He foretells that someone great
By the Father will be sent,
"He's the One you should await!"
Shouted John, "Now go repent!"

"His baptism is not like mine
Not with water, but with fire,
And with Spirit, pure, divine,
He's the Lord you should desire."

"I am not worthy to bow
To His feet to tie the strings.
I shall wait for Jesus now
He's the King of all the kings."

Then, the Lord Himself appears,
"Baptize Me," He says to John.
He cannot believe his ears!
"You should do it, You're the Son."

Jesus looked at John and said,
"To make things completely right,
You must do it. Go ahead."
He was baptized in God's sight.

When the Lord Jesus came out
After the baptism was done,
God's voice was heard all about,
"This is My beloved Son!"

Holy Spirit from above
Came down onto Him with might
In the shape of a white dove;
What a great, glorious sight!

In the desert wind and heat
Jesus later had to stay;
Forty days He did not eat,
Satan wanted Him to stray.

"Can You change these rocks to bread?"
Satan whispered in His ear.
"Do not tempt Me!" Jesus said,
And the devil disappeared.

Then Satan took Jesus to town
And they climbed the temple high,
"If You are the Son, jump down!"
"Do not test God!" Christ replied.

One more time the devil tried,
"Worship me and You will get
All the kingdoms long and wide
And Your needs will all be met."

"Go away from Me right now!"
Answered Jesus, "For you know
That, as written, I will bow
Only before God alone."

Satan went off in defeat
And the angels from above
Came down with great joy to greet
And to serve the Lord in love.

The Disciples

One day, on a nice, big lake,
Simon Peter cast his net
But he couldn't catch a break;
No fish for him, not just yet.

He's been fishing all day long
Casting here, and casting there,
Everything was going wrong.
"Where's the fish?" Peter despaired.

As he stood there looking grim
Jesus showed up on the beach;
"Take your boat," He said to him,
"Come with Me and see Me preach."

Jesus spoke to crowds ashore
As their teacher and their friend,
Peter paddled with an oar
Till the day came to an end.

When the preaching was all done
Jesus said, "Now cast the net."
"We will not catch even one!"
Answered Peter, "Want to bet?"

"Lord, I worked hard night and day
Fishing up and down the lake,
I don't think that we should stay,
It would be a big mistake."

Jesus answered, "You should try,"
And so as they calmly float
Peter raises the nets high,
And he throws them out the boat.

Peter can't believe his eyes!
The net fills with fish, and then
Jesus adds to his surprise
When He says, "You will fish for men."

Later, Jesus climbed a mount
His disciples joined Him too,
He gave blessings there to count
For all people, even you!

Jesus blessed those who were poor,
Those whose lives were very tough.
And He offered them His cure
Grace and faith – for that's enough.

Those who had a peaceful mind
Got a blessing from Him too,
And those who were pure and kind?
They would see God! Yes, it's true!

"You're this planet's salt and light,"
That's how Jesus spoke in love,
"Go and always do what's right,
Glorify your God above."

"I've not come to change God's plan
I've come to fulfill it, see.
I'm the only One who can
Do the work God gave to Me."

The disciples were in awe
By His words so wise and true,
When they heard Him they all saw
He came to make all things new.

The Miracles

In this story you will learn
Of the faith we should live by,
Which will teach us where to turn
When everything goes awry.

One day Jairus, a great dad
Ran to Jesus in distress
Because he was very sad
And he needed to be blessed.

His voice loudly filled the air,
"Lord, please help! I am in pain!
My dear child died!" He despaired.
"You can make her well again!"

When they got there, Jesus heard
People's cries and saw their tears.
They were waiting for His word,
Would He satisfy their ears?

"Go outside," Jesus commands,
"She's not dead, she's just asleep."
Shocked, the people wave their hands
Scoffing Him, they no more weep.

Jesus walks up to the bed,
Puts the dead girl's hand in His
And — oh my — she moves her head!
Now they know who Jesus is!

At another time we meet
Jesus teaching from His word
Suddenly out in the street,
Some strange noises can be heard.

A few friends carry a man
In a bed where he is laid;
They believe that Jesus can
Heal him as they all had prayed.

Big crowds gather round the scene,
The bed can't fit through the door!
Then, the men squeeze in between,
Through the roof to reach the floor.

Jesus sees that they believe
And He tells the man who's ill:
"My forgiveness now receive,
Trust Me, for this is God's will."

But the Pharisees are near
And they think Jesus is wrong,
For the Scripture's very clear:
To God forgiveness belongs.

"What is easier?" Jesus asks,
"To forgive sin or to heal?
Which of these important tasks
Would you choose? What do you feel?"

"I can both heal and forgive,"
Jesus looked at them and said,
"Watch Me heal this man! Believe!"
The sick man got out of bed!

People stared at him in shock,
He was ill, but now he's fine!
Thanks to Jesus he can walk,
This miracle was a sign!

The Friends of Jesus

Having friends is really great,
I am sure you will agree.
Jesus had them too, but wait!
Pay attention, and you'll see.

Bethany was a small town,
In which Lazarus was raised.
You should probably sit down,
This will make you so amazed!

One day Lazarus got ill,
So ill was he that he died!
His best friends' hearts became still,
As they buried him, they cried.

Jesus, when He learned the news,
Started walking right away.
There was not much time to lose,
Traveling must start today!

When He got there, things were bad,
His friend died four days before!
Everyone was very sad,
What could be done anymore?

Lazarus' dear sisters wept
When the Lord Himself arrived,
"Only You, Lord, could have kept
Our dear Lazarus alive!"

Jesus said, "Let it be known
That God's glory fills this place!
Now remove this big gravestone,
Let Me feel My friend's embrace!"

Then He loudly said, "Come out!"
And His friend came right outside!
People were shocked! Not a doubt!
God was surely glorified!

In this part we'll climb a tree
With Zacchaeus, a short man.
For God wanted him to see
That for him He had a plan.

The job that Zacchaeus had
Was to boss people around,
That's why he made others mad,
No one liked him in his town.

When he heard that Jesus came
To Jericho to spend time,
Zacchaeus was not ashamed,
A tall tree he quickly climbed.

Did he do it just for fun?
No! He simply was too small!
He could only see God's Son
From a tree branch, above all.

Jesus saw him and said, "Hey!
You can come down from that tree.
In your house I want to stay."
People thought, "How could that be?"

They were shocked that Jesus chose
This mean man to be His host.
But that's sometimes how it goes;
Mean people need God the most.

113

The Good Samaritan

One time Jesus met a man
Who said to Him, "My dear friend,
Please do tell me, if You can,
How to live without an end?"

"What does Holy Scripture say?"
Jesus asked him, "Do you know?
Do you read it every day?
Does it teach you how to grow?

Love your God, because He's good
With your whole heart, soul, and mind
Love your neighbor, like you should,
Be respectful and be kind."

But the young man says again,
"Tell me who my neighbor is."
Jesus says, "Let Me explain."
And the story goes like this:

This one Jew was on his way
Walking to a nearby town,
When some thugs ruined his day,
Stole his things and beat him down.

Hurt so badly he could die
He was lying on the ground,
Soon a priest came walking by
But decided to go round.

Then a Levite walked by too.
Did he stop to show some care?
Do you think he had a clue?
Maybe he was simply scared?

Then, another man came near
From Samaria, not a Jew.
He looked down and said, "Oh, dear,
There is something I must do!"

One thing you should know about
Both Samaritans and Jews,
Is that they could do without
Sharing one another's views.

But in spite of all the hate,
This Samaritan was good.
He helped the man in his state,
Doing everything he could.

He took care of his bruised skin,
Fed him, saved him from despair,
Took him to a nearby inn,
And then paid for his stay there.

Then the good Samaritan
Had to travel right ahead.
"Care for this man, if you can,"
To the innkeeper he said.

Then he paid him even more,
"Please, accept it. It's your earn.
Should it not cover your chores,
I will add when I return."

Now, please answer, if you can
Who's the neighbor? Who was fair?
It's the good Samaritan,
Because he took time to care.

The Parables

Do you know that Jesus told
Stories to teach things unseen?
Two of them I will unfold,
And then tell you what they mean.

The first parable compares
God's own kingdom to a field,
For which farmers deeply care
Working hard to see its yield.

One of them scattered some seeds
And then, tired, he went to bed.
Meanwhile his foe planted weeds,
Deep down in the soil they spread.

All the servants ran and cried,
"What a trouble! What a flop!
Will you let the good seeds die?
Why, do something, save the crop!"

"Listen well!" the sower said,
"Let them be and let them grow,
After harvest we will shred
All the bad ones that were sown.

Now, go gather all the wheat,
And burn all the weeds in fire.
Evil will suffer defeat,
For that is my deep desire."

It will surely be the same
When this world comes to an end;
All the sin and all the shame
To the fire will be sent.

God will judge and separate
Good from sin, both yours and mine,
Evil will see its ill fate;
And the righteous ones will shine.

In the story number two
You will hear this wondrous news:
God in heaven cares for you,
And that's something you can't lose!

Hundred sheep were grazing out
In the meadows of green bliss;
Could the shepherd do without
One if it had gone amiss?

Would he leave the ninety nine
And risk danger to find one
Until it was wholly fine?
Would he get this hard job done?

Other sheep are well behaved
Grazing in the pastures green.
Only one needs to be saved,
But it's nowhere to be seen!

The good shepherd stays on course
And at last the sheep is found!
He can go back and rejoice,
His whole flock is safe and sound.

May these stories make you wise,
While they teach you this great truth:
You are precious in God's eyes,
Follow Him throughout your youth.

There are many stories more
That the Lord told in His Word.
Some you may have read before,
Others are still to be heard.

But now put the book away
Close your eyes, turn off the light;
And do not forget to pray,
Have sweet dreams, my friend, good nig

The Storm

This new story is about
Faith, which matters to us all.
Let us read it and find out
That it can be big or small.

On a shiny, gorgeous lake
Some disciples board a boat,
For they have a trip to make,
And are now about to float.

With the sun now going down
They see someone walking by,
As though it was solid ground,
Even though the waves are high!

"It must be a ghost," they say.
Crouching in the boat with fear
They are more and more afraid
Of who's going to appear.

Suddenly they hear a voice
Coming to them loud and clear,
"It is I, don't fear, rejoice!"
Is it Jesus? Is He here?

Peter stands up to his feet
And says, "Lord, if it is You,
Let me walk to You and meet
For I want to try it too."

"Okay, Peter. Come on out,"
Jesus says and Peter goes.
But he's overcome with doubt
And his fear of drowning grows.

"Help me, Lord, I'm going down!"
The Lord's arm stops Peter's fall.
"Fear not, I won't let you drown,
Even though your faith is small."

On another dark late night
They are boating yet again,
On the open sea in spite
Of the coming storm and rain.

Clouds are heavy and they're black
The disciples fear the waves.
The Lord's sleeping in the back,
Will the sea become their graves?

"Wake up, Jesus, or we're dead!
Don't You see what's going on?"
The men panic, but instead
They should have faith in God's Son.

Jesus wakes up, sees their fear,
And rebukes the storm out loud.
Now the sea is calm and clear,
Not a single heavy cloud!

Then Jesus says this to His men,
"Have faith! Why do you still doubt?
I have shown you once again
What My power is about."

The disciples are in awe
Because Jesus calmed the sea,
And they know that what they saw
Will now help them to believe.

Forgiveness

Are there times when you are bad?
Times when you're up to no good?
Are your parents sometimes sad,
When you don't do what you should?

Those are perfect times to pray;
When you pray, you always win!
God will show you the right way,
He will save you from your sin.

You can tell God what you've done
Do it with a humble heart,
He forgives you through His Son,
Giving you a brand-new start!

You can know that this is true
For the Bible does not lie,
Here's a story just for you,
Things to cherish and live by.

A young lady was once caught
Breaking an important rule;
To the temple she was brought
By a crowd whose plan was cruel.

She sinned badly, that's a fact,
Her own husband she betrayed.
And they caught her in the act
Now the price had to be paid.

Jesus was asked by the crowd
What her punishment should be.
"If you're perfect," He said out loud,
"Hit her with a stone, feel free."

One by one they left in shame,
And the girl got off the floor.
"To forgive and love I came,"
Jesus said, "Go sin no more."

The next story shows you that
Loving dads always forgive,
Even when you are a brat,
They have tender hearts to give.

Once a son said to his dad,
"I want to be really free,
Give me money, don't be sad,
Say goodbye and let me be."

This request broke his dad's heart
But he did it for his son.
"Take this money. It's your part."
"Thanks," the son said and was gone.

The boy's journey did not last,
All he did was have wild fun.
He spent all his money fast,
Now his free life was all done.

He was hungry, he was poor,
He thought, "It would be so sweet
To return home, that's for sure,
Where there's always food to eat."

Quickly, he made up his mind,
And he traveled back in shame
Thinking, "Will my dad be kind?
Will he be glad that I came?"

When he finally got near,
His dad saw him and he ran,
"My son! I'm so glad you're here!
Now I am a happy man!"

The whole house was full of joy
For the lost son has been found!
He was once a foolish boy,
But forgiveness brought him round.

Jesus
and the Children

Everywhere that Jesus went
People followed, big and small;
That's because the Lord was sent
To teach, bless, and save us all.

One day five thousand or so
Gathered round Him, children too.
But the food supply was low,
What will the disciples do?

First they whine and do it loud,
"Lord, there is no food to eat!"
Jesus said, "We'll feed this crowd.
All their needs we'll surely meet."

What would then be the main dish?
Only one boy brought some bread,
Five loaves of it, and two fish;
Can this little food be spread?

Jesus called the little boy
Asked him to share what he brought,
Blessed the food and said, "Enjoy!"
Everybody ate a lot!

When they gathered all the crumbs
There were twelve baskets in all!
Such miracles only come
When on God Himself we call.

Other kids loved Jesus, too
When He taught, they would attend.
For they found him to be true,
And they knew He was their friend.

The disciples sometimes frowned
When some parent brought their child;
They did not want kids around,
Because things could be quite wild.

"Don't forbid the kids to come,"
Jesus had to make it clear,
"Let them listen, they're not dumb,
And they also want to hear."

"You should also be like them
And trust every word I say,
Or you won't know who I am,
And you just might go astray."

Jesus paused, then spoke again,
"Be like little kids, My dear,
Life eternal you will gain
Turn to Me, and have no fear."

That's what Jesus had to say
About children and their worth.
Do you realize that He has prayed
For you since your very birth?

He wants you to live for Him
And be safe forevermore,
Free from sadness, fear, and sin,
He is knocking on your door.

You can open even now,
If you do it, you are smart.
Want to live? He'll show you how,
Just invite Him into your heart.

In Jerusalem

In Jerusalem today
There is singing in the air;
It's a very festive day,
Lots of people everywhere.

Streets are filled from end to end,
Much joy, happiness and fun;
For the Lord came to attend
And bring hope to everyone!

The good news is spreading fast,
Everybody wants to see;
Jesus came to them at last
All the way from Galilee!

Do you know on what He rode?
On a donkey, of all things!
Praise from all the people flowed,
He was treated like a king.

God had promised long ago
To the nation that He chose
A new King that they would know;
Now He's there, so very close.

"Praise, Hosanna!" people shout,
"Son of David, save us please!"
Some joyfully jump about,
Others get down on their knees.

From the streets Lord Jesus went
To a very special place
Called a temple, which is meant
To worship and give Him praise.

What Jesus saw there was not good,
People did not pray at all;
They did not act like they should
And the place was like a mall!

Little booths and shopping stalls,
It looked like a busy fair!
Buyers, sellers filled the halls
For God's house they did not care.

Jesus quickly looked around
He was angry, and He grieved,
Turned the tables upside down
And told everyone to leave.

"This is My house! Not a shop!
It's a place to come and pray!
All of this has got to stop,
Take this merchandise away!"

From that time on, Jesus taught
At the temple day and night.
People heard and learned a lot,
Thanks to Him lives were made right.

But there were some Pharisees
Who were sowing hate and doubt,
And they were not very pleased,
So they wanted Jesus out.

You will soon discover more
Things that will be sad but true.
There is tragedy in store,
Jesus dies for me and you.

The Last Supper

The Lord Jesus and His men
Were preparing for a feast,
Celebrating the times when
Jewish people were released.

For they used to work as slaves
In the far Egyptian land,
But God showed them that He saves,
They have seen His mighty hand.

When they sat down to the meal,
Jesus looked around and said,
"What I'll tell you now is real,
One of you, men, wants Me dead."

"Who might that be, Lord? Not me!"
All of them sadly replied.
Jesus answered, "Watch and see,
He's sitting by My side."

Judas was the very man
Whom the Lord just pointed to;
He got up, then left and ran,
That is all that he could do.

Jesus took bread in His hand
Saying, "It's My flesh, you see;
I give you a new command,
Eat it and remember Me."

Then He lifted a big cup
Asking His men to obey.
"It's My blood, so drink it up,
It will wash your sins away."

These are symbols to remind
The whole world of what He has done.
He died to save all mankind
And He still loves everyone.

Let us now learn more about
Judas, who betrayed the Lord,
Selling his great Teacher out
And accepting a reward.

What he did was very bad,
He sold Jesus to His foes,
Left the only friends he had,
That's the tragic life he chose!

Was Judas always a bad man?
Only God knows if it's true;
Did he always have this plan?
That is something God knows, too.

We do know that in the past
He was one of the Lord's friends,
But his friendship didn't last
Now he cannot make amends.

It's too late, what's done is done,
He got money for his deed,
Evil men captured God's Son,
Judas satisfied his greed.

Thirty silver coins he got
For the selling of his friend,
And his awful, sinful plot
Brought about a tragic end.

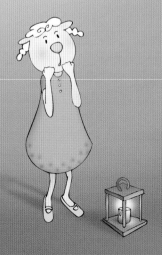

Gethsemane

On a quiet, starry night
Jesus wished to be away
At a place which was just right,
To be quiet and to pray.

His friends also came along
To this olive grove in town,
For they wanted to be strong
Hoping not to let Him down.

"Stay alert and pray for Me,"
Jesus asked them at that place
Which was called Gethsemane;
They saw sadness on His face.

Jesus got down on His knees
With a heavy heart He prayed,
"O, My Father will You please
Help Me and come to My aid?

Take this suffering away
If at all it can be done.
But if not, I will obey
Because I am Your true Son."

Meanwhile, Jesus' friends closed their eyes
Sleeping calmly on the ground
Jesus saw them and said, "Rise!"
They woke up hearing that sound.

Three more times He had to speak
Trying to wake up His men
Who were willing, but so weak
That they fell asleep again.

But they should have been alert
When their Lord was in distress.
When He suffered and felt hurt
They should pray more and sleep less.

Suddenly, lights filled the night
On the road to the grove's gate;
Angry people full of spite
Shouting loudly words of hate.

Judas was in charge of this!
He ran to the Lord and then
Greeted Him with a fake kiss,
Showing Him to evil men.

Now the turmoil has begun
They came to arrest the Lord!
Peter wouldn't be outdone
And he reached to get his sword.

With it, he cut off the ear
Of a servant who was there.
Jesus, who was very near
Told Peter he was unfair.

Then Jesus placed the man's ear back,
"Do not use your sword!" He said,
"If with sword you will attack,
From the sword you will be dead."

Then Jesus said, "Do what you must."
They were ready to begin
Doing that which was unjust,
They jailed Him who knew no sin.

Lonely Jesus

It is sad to write about
Things which happen in this part,
But they cannot be left out
For they show God's loving heart.

Jesus was now in the hands
Of a priest who wanted to
Meet the angry crowd's demands,
And that's what he planned to do.

Meanwhile, Peter told His friend,
"Lord, I'll give my life for You!
I'll be with You till the end!"
Will he really follow through?

Jesus answered Peter's pride,
"Peter, it will not be so,
Three times I will be denied
Before morning roosters crow."

"I won't leave You! I am strong!
I can do it!" Peter thought.
But soon things turned very wrong
And he feared he would be caught.

When the people saw his face
They said, "You knew Jesus, too!"
He denied, what a disgrace!
Peter petered out. Would you?

Then Peter heard the rooster crow
And he realized what he'd done.
Bitter tears began to flow
Down his sad face, one by one.

At this time Jesus was jailed
By those who wished He would die.
They accused Him, but they failed
To prove that He'd ever lied.

An important priest was there;
He said, "Tell me, or just nod
That is, Jesus, if You dare,
Did You really come from God?"

"Yes, I did," replied the Lord.
The priest raised his hands up high,
"This claim cannot be ignored!
He's a liar! He must die!"

Then they dragged Him yet again
To the governor's abode,
Because it was through his reign
That the death could be bestowed.

But the governor could see
No wrongdoing in this case.
"He's not guilty, let Him be,"
He told them to leave his place.

When they heard it, they got loud,
"You must punish Him," they said.
"Crucify Him!" yelled the crowd,
"He's no God! He must be dead!"

Scorned, despised, and all alone
The Lord was sentenced to die.
Although He came to His own,
His teaching they did deny.

The Sacrifice

The Lord Jesus was betrayed,
Beaten, mocked, misunderstood;
His weak body was then laid
On a large cross made of wood.

On that very cross He died,
Killed by people full of hate.
Those who loved Him watched and cried;
Others joked about His fate.

His cross was placed in between
Two mean thugs who broke the law,
Even though His heart was clean
And it didn't have a flaw.

Jesus died there for you and me
And for everyone on earth.
His cross means we can be free
To experience a new birth.

For God loved this world so much
That He gave His only Son,
And His sacrifice was such
That it could save everyone.

When He died, the darkness fell
On the land and all its parts,
Then the earth shook in its shell
And fear entered people's hearts.

Those who loved Him till the end
Took His body off the cross;
In the tomb they laid their friend
And placed a huge stone across.

Does the story end right here?
Should we stop reading and grieve?
No! There is much more to hear!
And it's so hard to believe!

Two days and two nights went past
And then the third morning came.
There is some good news at last,
Something awesome to proclaim!

Women came to the Lord's tomb
On the morning of that day,
They brought spices and perfume
But the stone was rolled away!

Where was Jesus? Not inside!
They could not believe their eyes,
Was He stolen? Did He hide?
What a strange, shocking surprise!

Suddenly, they saw a light
Deep inside the tomb's abyss;
It's an angel, all in white!
When he saw them he said this:

"You seek Jesus, I suppose?
Go now and tell everyone
He's not here for He arose!
God gave life back to His Son!"

Isn't this news really great?
The Lord Jesus lives again!
His death opened heaven's gate,
When He rose, we all have gained.

The Lord's work was now complete
He changed sorrow into joy,
For death suffered a defeat
And its power was destroyed.

Jesus died for me and you,
We gained, when He suffered loss.
Now the best thing we can do
Is to go and preach the cross.

The Comforter

Because the Lord Jesus rose
He now lives among us all,
Where we go, He also goes
And He helps us not to fall.

When it happened, the news spread
Through the land and all its parts,
"Jesus lives! He is not dead!"
Gladness entered His friends' hearts.

He had walked for many days
Teaching them His Father's will,
And His holy, perfect ways
He Himself came to fulfill.

Then He told them, "I must go
To My Father's house again.
You won't be forsaken, though,
My work will not be in vain.

Holy Spirit will arrive,
He will make you strong and bold
To spread good news and revive
Souls of those who will be told."

Jesus finished and right then
He was taken to the sky.
Looking up, His faithful men
Worshiped Him and waved goodbye.

The disciples now would wait
For the promise to come true,
It would happen on the date
Known as Pentecost to you.

When that day finally came
They were gathered in one place;
Praying and praising God's name
There was hope on every face.

Suddenly, like Jesus said,
Holy Ghost came down with fire;
Which was placed above each head,
A bright flame by God inspired.

A miracle happened then,
Though different tongues they knew,
Everyone could understand
And speak to each other, too!

Others watching the whole scene
Asked themselves, "What is this for?
We have never, ever seen
Anything like that before!"

Peter got up and he spoke
To those who were standing near.
"What you're seeing is no joke!
Come on closer, lend your ear.

Things the prophets have foretold
Which you surely read about,
Are now about to unfold
When the Spirit is poured out."

From that day on, until now,
People carry the good news.
And you too can ask God how
He can put you to His use.